It's All In Your Struggle!

Copyrighted 2024 by Neshell Surfaith Montgomery

Printed in the United States of America. All rights reserved under International Copyright Law. Contents and /or cover may not be reproduced in whole or in part in any form without the written consent of Neshell Surfaith Montgomery. You may contact the author at heavensmydestiny05@yahoo.com

IT'S ALL IN YOUR STRUGGLE

BY 1ST LADY NESHELL SURFAITH MONTGOMERY

ACKNOWLEDGEMENTS

First, I give honor to God and to Jesus Christ and the Holy Spirit who has guided me in writing these articles of faith. I give special thanks to by husband and Pastor Charles G. Montgomery who has supported and encouraged me. I give thanks to my family and friends who told me that I can do it and said things like "Girl you know you got this". I would love to give a special thanks to Prophet and Prophetess Rodney and Regina Jiles who told me that God said that I was going to write a book and it has come to pass. I dedicate the articles in this book to my mother and father, Willie and Pearline Smith and my sisters Paulette Smith and Josephine Smith and my brother Willie C. Smith whom all have transitioned to Glory!

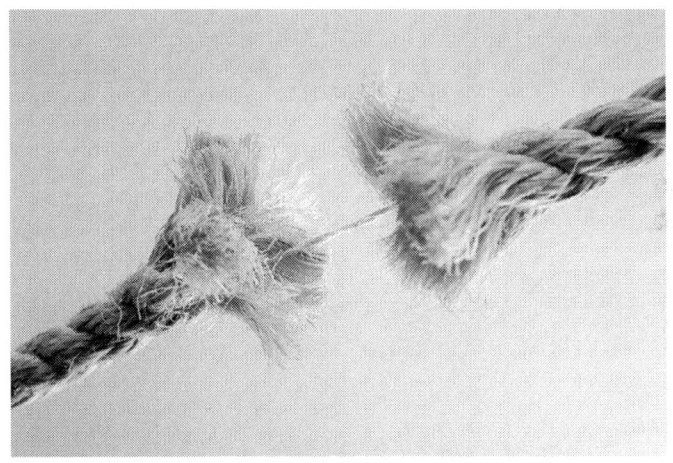

Table of Contents

Volume 1

1. A DESPERATE CRY/BE REAL WITH GOD
2. A FIGHT WITH YOUR NAME ON IT
3. GETTING INTO YOUR QUITE PLACE
4. GOING BEYOND YOUR BLESSING
5. IT'S ABOUT TO GO DOWN
6. IT'S ALL IN YOUR STRUGGLE
7. IT'S TIME TO FIGHT
8. IT'S TIME TO PUT YOUR MOUNTAIN IN CHECK
9. IT'S VACCINATION TIME
10. LET THE SERVICE BEGIN

Volume 2

11. ME AND MY BIG MOUTH
12. ON THE EDGE
13. PRISONER OF BITTERNESS
14. SHIFTED WHILE IN THE PROCESS
15. STOP THE ABORTION

16. WHAT BATTLE ARE YOU FIGHTING

17. WHAT WATER HAVE YOU BEEN DRINKING? BECAUSE IT'S IN THE WATER!

18. WHEN GOD IS WITH YOU

19. YOU DON'T KNOW THE COST OF MY PRAISE

20. DON'T ALLOW YOUR FAILURES TO STOP YOU FROM SERVING GOD

21. DON'T COUNT ME OUT JUST YET

Introduction

At some point in your life, you, like many others, have had to struggle. A struggle is a forceful or violent effort to do something, or to get free from something. A person can struggle getting a job or buying a house or car. A person can struggle being in a toxic marriage or relationship. Struggling can take the face of many things. The word struggle has such a disdain against it. Struggling is the thing that many people look down on people for, but everyone does. Everyone in this lifetime has struggled in some way or another. I struggled so much, that I began to question God. I asked God why I experienced so much struggle in my life. That is when the Lord began to deal with me about struggling.

The Lord let me know that I am not the only one who've struggled with some things in my life. The Lord also let me know that no one stays the same after a struggle. A struggle has a way of changing a person; either for the good or for the bad. You can rest assure that after one has struggled through something that they are not the same. The Lord did not allow me to stay in a 'pity party' too long. The Lord called me out of that low place and gave me language for my struggle. The Lord told me that for where he was taking me that I needed to be strong. Struggle has a way of strengthening you.

When you struggle with something you begin to pull on strength that you did not know you had. When you struggle with something you begin to realize your creative ability. I will liken it to someone who cooks from scratch. A person who cooks from scratch knows how to substitute for certain ingredients. A person who cooks from scratch knows how to create/make a meal at home that they did not buy from the Fast-Food restaurant but it taste just as good.

God told me that I was his warrior. God said when a butterfly is in the cocoon he is being made. The cocoon struggles to get out and when it does it is so beautiful and strong. God then showed me a giant bible and it open up to the center and he laid me in the middle and cover me with each page. I was fully covered in the word of God and he said when he finish with me that I was going to be beautiful and strong.

Volume #1

Issue #1

A DESPERATE CRY / BEING REAL WITH GOD

At this point in my life, I have learned something very important. I learned that God is still making me and improving me and leading me. There are still so many things in my life that I have to learn. No matter how old you get, there will always be room to learn more. With God there is always a learning process so that you can continue to progress in your life.

We can't stay the same with God but without God we stay the same. Real change comes from having God in your life and being yielded to him. If not we become stagnated like a lake with no movement. No life and all green and yucky. I have seen a lot of lakes without any motion and it begins to build dirt and becomes unsanitary water. Lakes naturally have slower water flow than rivers. Consequently, because of the slow motion, it gives time for build up of algae bloom and waterborne illnesses. If there are any fish in a lake like that it may not be safe to eat.

Let's talk about being real with ourselves for a second and being real with God. Every day of our lives we go through different situations and different circumstances. Different trials and different problems. As a result of these things we become stressed out. We become sad, angry and even depressed at times. During these times we try to fix things ourselves but that has never worked. Things only get worse and not better. We then allow pride to come in and it keeps us from asking for help. Pride will keep you from reaching out for help even when help is accessible to you. Pride will cause you to think that people are against you when they are actually for you. Pride will cause you to think that people just want to know your business. Pride will cause you to not want to be transparent and accountable to anyone to receive the appropriate assistance that you may need in life. Over the course of time your situation grows worse because you did not address it. Then the frustration kicks in with life. We are frustrated because we see the opposite of what we preached about. We see the opposite of what our faith says and we feel as if God did not answer our prayer.

The book of James 4:8 Tells us to draw nigh to God and God will draw nigh unto us. We have to get closer to God and he will become closer to us. We have to learn how to cry out and be real with God and he will be real with us. Just like a mother knows her child's cry when its real and when its not; likewise with God. He knows our cry! God knows when we are at the point of desperation.

God knows when we are not truly sincere with him, especially if our actions do not show our sincerity.

We have to let pride go so that we can be delivered. In Psalm 51 King David cries out to God in repentance. David understood that even though he was a King that he was not perfect and that there were some areas in his life where he had lived in error. David was honest with himself and God. David asked God to give him a clean heart. That is what we all need, is a clean heart. If you recognize areas in your life where you have errored, just repent to God and ask him for a clean heart.

In the book of Genesis 32 Jacob became so desperate that he refused to let the angel of the Lord go until he blessed him. The struggle became so intense that Jacob's thigh was knocked out of socket.

> But Jacob stayed behind by himself, and a man wrestled with him until daybreak. When the man saw that he couldn't get the best of Jacob as they wrestled, he deliberately threw Jacob's hip out of joint. The man said, "Let me go; it's daybreak." Jacob said, I'm not letting you go til you bless me." The man said, "What's your name?" He answered, Jacob. The man said, But no longer. Your name is no longer Jacob. From now on it's Israel (God-Wrestler); you've wrestled with God and you've come through.
>
> (Genesis 32:24-28 MSG)

Jacob's level of desperation altered his physical body. Jacob's hip was knocked out of joint. That puts Jacob in excruciating pain. Yet Jacob held on until the angel of the Lord responded to him in favor. We need to hold on to God until we get the response that is needed. Some of us give up too easily and resort to other vices. Stop giving yourself options. Christ is the only way!

In the book of Jonah, Jonah tried giving himself an option outside of what God had instructed him to do. Jonah found himself in the belly of a whale. Disobedience will put you in places that God did not authorize. That makes you vulnerable to danger.

Don't be ashamed to cry out to God. God wants and expects for us to cry out to him when we are in need. The Apostle Paul said: "For I am not ashamed of the gospel of Christ: for it is the power of God unto salvation to everyone that believeth; to the Jew first, and also to the Greek." Romans 1:16.

Issue #2

A Fight with your name on it

"A fight that has been assigned to you"

Scripture: 2nd Corinthians 10:1-5

Today I come with a message of encouragement and hope because God has called us to be overcomers and not quitters. I heard a slogan that said; "Quitters never win and winners never quit". The topic that God has given me for such a time as this is; "A Fight with your name on it and a fight that has been assigned to you.

A **Fight** is a physical struggle between two opposing individuals or groups, battles, conflict.

Assign is to give out, Distribute, (2) To select for duty or office, appoint and designate

God knows just what we need to get us to our destination. God knows what it takes to get us out of our comfort zone. He knows how high to turn up the heat, to cause us to move and get in high gear because sometimes we want to quit. Some of us want to throw in the towel and just give up. God is saying know because he has assigned this fight just for you. God is saying that he is the assigner of this fight, the I AM. The Lord says that he has placed your name on this ballet.

GOD:

Remember the prayer request that you put before me when you laid at the alter? Do you remember when you cried out and asked me to save you? Remember what you asked me in your secret closet, that you desired to be more like me? Stop getting angry because the I AM is here! I am honoring your prayer requests. I heard you and I assigned you this fight, to get you to the place where I need you to be. Stop blaming the devil. You are giving him to much credit. I AM THE I AM, with all power in my hands! I want you out of your comfort zone because it is not good for you. You can't make any progress there. You cannot move forward there. It's time for you to get off the milk and chew on some solid food. The fights that I assign to you will make you stronger and wiser.

The assigned fights that God has assigned to you are as follows:

1. The fight of trusting Him! You have to study Psalm 4:5, 7:1, 37:3, 62:8 and 71:1. This fight will truly teach you how to trust God.

2. The fight of loving Him! You have to study Psalm 18:1, Proverbs 10:12, Matthew 5:43-44, Matthew 22:37, and John 14:15. This fight will help you love God more than anyone or anything.

3. The fight of obeying Him! You have to study Zechariah 6:15, Jeremiah 7:23, Isaiah 15:22, Deuteronomy 30:8, 28:1-14, 28:15-68. This fight will teach you how to always obey God.

When God assign you these fights; know that you are never alone. In Hebrews 13:5, God said that he will never leave you nor forsake you. You can fight the good fight of faith and be the winner and champion God is calling you to be. Come and let's give the devil a black eye and bloody nose and some bruises ribs! Lets ask God to continue to prepare us for the fights that he has assigned us. On this journey, sometimes friends can't help you, crying won't help you, running won't help you and feeling sorry for yourself won't help you. This is your fight that the I AM has assigned to you and he is the only one that can cause you to win and be the champion in his Kingdom.

Issue #3

Getting into your quiet place

"But thou, when thou prayest, enter into thy closet, and when thou hast shut thy door, pray to thy Father which is in secret; and thy Father which seeth in secret shall reward thee openly."
(Matthew 6:6)

Jesus understood the intentionality of going to a secret place to commune with God. Jesus had multitudes following him and he had to be purposeful and skillful in getting to a quiet place to pray. It is the same way with us. Everything is campaigning for our attention and it is important that we make time for God. We need God to reveal to us, next steps for our lives.

Jesus knows the value of a quiet place. A quiet place is a time for prayer. A time to get away from the cares of everyday life. We live in a world that is filled with many distractions, disturbances and interruptions. We all need a quiet place to go to so we can hear from God. There we can allow our hearts to open up and search for a deeper spiritual connection. In the cares of this world we can sometime feel like we are drowning and we need to come up for some fresh air. A noisy place drowns out the voice of God. God is speaking to us but we can't hear him because of all the noise that is surrounding us! The noise of lies, the noise of pain, the noise of stress, the noise of confusion, the noise of deceitfulness, the noise of unforgiveness, the noise of hurt and the noise of felling all alone. There is so much noise that I cannot name them all but God knows them all.

In your quiet place is where you can always find God. He is always waiting for you there. God will never leave us and he will never forsake us. God will always be there with his arms wide open so we can just fall into them and what a sweet and awesome peace filled with nothing but love there.

I am talking about a giant relief in your spirit. That is why I love God so much! God is our quiet place and he is always listening. Praise God! There is one thing to tell you about what something you heard or read but I have experienced God for myself and this is pouring out of my own private times with God. I know for fact that God is there and will always be there. You should try him in that way. He will be there every time. He is waiting on us to come to him.

There are many experiences I can share about my quiet moments with God. There was one time when I felt alone and abandoned. I felt like I had no one to talk to or trust. Negative interactions with people had caused me not to trust anyone with my heart. I was in so much pain and my soul was hurting very deeply. I had to find my way to God/to a quiet place where I can commune with him. My heart began to race and it was as if I was having an anxiety attack. I could not breathe. I had a flood of tears coming down my face. When I opened my mouth to cry out to God, He heard me. I could feel his presence come in the room. Then I began to feel an overwhelming feeling of comfort. The Lord himself began to comfort me.

    There is nothing like the love of God holding you close to him, protecting you and giving you peace all at the same time. Then feeling yourself breathe again. I don't mind giving God all of the praise! Being in a quiet place will restore you in every area of your life. It is simply taking time out to communicate with God. It is crucial for us to maintain a healthy, spiritual, emotional, physical life with God. He will lead and guide us. We need this quiet place to reenergize and find strength to deal with daily challenges. Even Jesus would go to a quiet place to talk with his Father! Only the presence of the Lord can renew, restore, revitalize, reinvigorate and reestablish our spirit. Only the spirit of God can cause you to breather again and cause dry bones to rise again! Being in your quiet place will allow God to do deep work on the inside of you. Being in your quiet place will allow you to be naked before the Lord. There God will strengthen us to resist the devil.

Issue #4

Going beyond your blessings

Blessings- Divine Favor, Something which provides happiness, prosperity or approval or a wish for good fortune or success.

Beyond- On or to the farther side of, out of the reach, more than, over and above.

We all enjoy receiving blessings from God. If we say that we don't, we are lying to ourselves. There is nothing wrong with receiving blessings from God. As a matter of fact, Jesus said: If ye abide in me, and my words abide in you, ye shall ask what ye will, and it shall be done unto you (John 15:7).

IT'S A DONE DEAL

God has been dealing with me about a certain issue. I had been pondering on some things and I began to question God about them. The Lord lead me to the book of Hosea 4:6. God began to tell me how the people of God are destroyed for the Lack of Knowledge.

He said too long, the church has prayed for a deeper experience with God but has stopped at the point of blessings and have not engaged in a spiritual relationship with God. Fellowship and relationship was the point of the sacrifice of the Son!

We the church have lost sight of this somehow and we must get it back. We must go beyond the blessing to engaging in fellowship and relationship with the blesser. The blessing should only be a byproduct of having a relationship with God. God wants us to know that there is so much more than material things. Acts 1:8 says that we shall receive power after that the Holy Ghost has come upon us. This same Dunamis power is the same power that Jesus the Christ operated in when he healed the sick, raised the dead, cleansed the lepers and so much more. We have to think on that level in order to operate and function on that level. We have to go beyond the blessing.

God wants us to walk in a new rhythm of miracles, a new rhythm of victory and a new rhythm of living. We have to go beyond and heal the sick and cast out devils in Jesus name. God said it's time to walk in your destiny and not in fear. He said he wants you to become strong and not weak.

God said this world needs more today. When we go beyond the blessings God will give us the ability to witness and to lead people to a life changing experience with Jesus. Oh…how awesome that will be! We need to stop short-changing ourselves with just the blessings of the Lord and go beyond and walk in the power of God. God said it is time to get out of your comfort zone and take a leap of faith and go beyond the blessings.

Issue #5

It's About to Go Down

SCRIPTURE: JOSHUA 11: 4-9

    The devil has attacked many of us. In different ways. At times he comes so often until it is hard to catch our breath. Just when you think you have conquered in one thing, here goes something else. That is why the bible says, ye in all these things we are more than conquerors. It takes more than just conquering a thing. We have to overcome it. We have to overcome, to the point where when it comes again, it will have no effect on us. We will be focused on the will of God for our lives. The enemy will whisper enticing things in our ears but to no avail because we have set our affections on things above and not things of this world.

The enemy wants you to quit and give up. As long as you are in this earth suit the devil will take occasion to distract you; but you have to have a made-up mind. I need you to look at the enemy and tell him in your loud, powerful voice; "It's about to go down".

See people of God we have purpose and a destiny. God is trying to get us to our destiny and purpose but the enemy does not want us to reach it. The enemy plays with our minds and cause us to doubt God and lose faith. We need to stop listening to the enemy and tell him it's about to go down!

God is saying It's about to go down, and he is commanding us to get up and fight. We can't get comfortable where we are. How are we going to reach our destiny if we don't move? God is saying get up from here and prepare yourselves for war, because its about to go down!

Joshua 11:4-9 was talking about a man who took Moses place. Moses lead the children of Israel out of Egyptian captivity. Moses was supposed to bring the children into the Promise Land but he was not the one to do that because of his disobedience. The mantle was placed on Joshua and it was him who brought the children of Israel over the river of Jordan into the Promised Land.

Can I let you in on a little secret? There is always eyes on your stuff and your promises. Don't allow the enemy to steal from you because God gave it to you. We have to get up and possess our stuff. If we don't move the enemy will take what belongs to us.

Allow me to share something with you about that passage of scripture. At that time Israel were already considered the underdog of the situation.

People of God, at times that is how we as believers as seen. The underdog or the least valued. The odds are stacked against us and the enemy thinks that he has us right where he wants us. So, you need to look within yourself and find the courage and the strength to say devil it is about to go down!

See all these Kings got together to come against Joshua with all their horses and chariots and armies. I know in their hearts they thought this was a win, win situation! Do you ever wonder why the enemy comes against you so much? Perhaps it is because God has favored you so much. The devil is jealous of that. God told Joshua to go and fight. Joshua didn't even wait for the armies to start. Joshua charged at them first. I want to leave you with three things to do before a fight.

1.) Obey your commander. God told Joshua to cut the hamstrings of the horses and set the chariots on fire and to take their swords and kill all of them!
2.) Don't hesitate! If you hesitate you will become afraid and won't move. You know since we are the underdogs, I thought about what kind of dog would I be? I chose to be a german shepherd because they are loyal, smart, loving and they are protectors. Come'on people of God, let's put our dog faces on and let our sharp teeth show and let

our growls be heard. Let's get ready to charge toward the enemy because it is about to go down.

3.) Go and pursue and take back what is rightfully ours! We have to stop allowing the

enemy to steal what God has given us. It's ours for the taking. I remember this story about this baby bear out by the lake trying to catch him some fish and all the sudden this big lion appeared and was trying to catch the baby bear but you know what that baby was not afraid and stood with his paws up growling going toward the lion and the lion turn to run away from the baby bear. That made the baby bear feel so proud but what the baby bear did not know was that his big papa bear was standing right behind him. That is all God wants us to do. He wants us to get out of our comfort zone and prepare ourselves for war. It's time for us to move toward the enemy and make the enemy run from us. God wants us to trust in him and know he has our backs because its about to go down!!

Issue #6
It's all in your struggle

At one point in my life, I struggled in prayer and felt as if I was not getting through to God. I began to ask God; how long will I continue without breakthrough? The Lord answered and said to me "It's All in Your Struggle"! I didn't get it at first, so I asked God what do you mean? I felt as if I had suffered enough. I began to say things like, God what are you saying to me? The pain that I was feeling was nothing to joke about and I was tired of suffering. I felt like a prisoner inside my own body and then all of a sudden I felt the presence of the Lord. I felt God's presence standing right in front of me. God said to me; Shut up, dry those tears and listen to me. He said I have purpose for you, and I can't have you weak.

God said you are my warrior. You have to be bold and strong to stand against the enemy. It's all in your struggle! So I began to prepare myself to study God's Word. Now the first thing I did was to look up the word 'Struggle'. Struggle means to be forceful; a violent effort to get free of restraints or resist attacks. You're trying to get free from something that is holding you back. There are a lot of things that hold us back and we all know who sends those things to us to stop us in our tracks and bring fear upon us. When fear is upon us we won't move forward in God.

What does the Word of God tell us about fear? 2nd Timothy 1:17 says; 'For God has not given us the spirit of fear but of power and of love and a sound mind'. So we have no business to be afraid and running from the devil! The devil should be running from us. When you rise up in the morning and your feet hit the floor, those devils should be running and saying 'oh he/she is and hauling out of your home.

Allow me to express to you that God has purpose for your pain! God wants us to stop despising our pain and praise in the midst of our pain. We have to stop acting like it's not normal to struggle because it's a part of life! God has a reason for your struggles and a reward for your faithfulness. Amen! Hebrews 11:6 tells us that It's impossible to please God without faith. So our pain has purpose and our faith will help us to get to that purpose because it's all in your struggle.

God said in Joshua 1:9, 'Have not I Commanded thee? Be strong and of good courage, be not afraid. Neither be thou dismayed for the Lord thy God is with thee withersoever thou goest. And also God tells us that no weapon that is formed against you will be able to prosper. So there is no need for us to be afraid of anything; It's All In Your Struggle.

Now that our eyes are open, allow me to share something with you that was impactful to me. 2nd Corinthinas 12:10 says: that God takes pleasure in infirmities, in reproaches, in necessities, in persecution, in distresses for Christ's sake; For when I am weak, then I am strong. Then God really began to show me what he meant about being in a struggle. Tears literally began to run down my face because of the visions that God began to share with me.

I love Butterfly's and that is something that not many people know about me. God asked me if I knew how butterfly's come to be so beautiful? Then the Lord told me that it was because of their struggle. When they are in the cocoon, they are going through a process which is going to get them to their purpose and they cannot get to their purpose without a struggle.

Struggle helps them build muscles, strength, beauty, boldness and power!

Then God showed me a vision of a giant bible and he opened the bible right in the middle so there was the same amount of pages on each side. Then with his big hands he placed me in the center and began to over lap the pages over me from the right to the left until I was covered with all of the pages of His Word. He said you are in my process and I have great purpose for you my daughter and I know my process has been hard on you and it has cause you to struggle and daughter it is pleasing me to see your struggle because I know the plans I have for you. Plans to prosper you and not to harm you and plans to give you home and a future! So daughter of mines, continue to be patient, continue to trust me, continue to be obedient, continue to endure. Continue to believe in me and when you come out of the struggle, you will be that beautiful butterfly that your father created and you shall fly and be free!

Issue #7

IT'S TIME TO FIGHT!
(SCRIPTURE : 1SAMUEL 17 : 45 – 51)

After studying this passage and going through some rough painful ordeals in life and the battles that were all around me, I decided it was time to fight! God began to minister to me. He allowed me to see the big picture. He even gave more than one topic to write from this passage. God said this is one passage but there are many messages in it. I began to see me in this passage and how there were so many enemies all around me. Then I looked at how David just, a little boy stood against the giant and defeated him. Why? Because David had some awesome faith in God. He said if God has protected him from the lion and the bear, God will protect him from the giant. In this God is showing us that it is time to fight. God is asking us a question: Where is our faith in Him? God moves according to our faith. Hebrews 11:6 says that without faith it is impossible to please God. We cannot expect God to move on our behalf if we do not have faith in him.

Ephesians 6:11 tells us to put on the whole armor of God, that we may be able to stand against the wiles of the devil. This is not time for self-pity and feeling sorry for yourself but it is time to fight. God is asking us where is our sword and why aren't we using it? God said stop trying to fight the enemy with our fists because we will never win that way. He said to use our sword that he has given us. We have to stop laying our sword down on the table, or on the shelf. Stop leaving it in the closet, in the trunk of our cars, packed down in boxes and only used for decorations. It's time to pick up our sword, dust it off, shine it up and begin to use it to fight the enemy. God is giving us the go ahead to sound the alarm and warn his people that it is time to fight. God said go and pursue the enemy with the Word of God. Go! No more running from the enemy. Come from behind those closed doors and take the sword of God and fight. Stop feeling sorry for yourself and fight. It is time to take our children back from the streets and from gangs and gang activity. We have to pick up our sword and command the enemy in Jesus name to loose our children. They don't belong to the enemy, they belong to God. Get up my brothers and sisters and fight because there is a work going on. We have to fight in Jesus name. Remember David, the little Shepherd boy? He heard the threats of the giant and he knew Saul's army were hiding from the giant. How many of you know that there is going to come a time that we can no longer hide? While the giant was slandering the name of the Israelites God, David said its time to fight. David refused to standby and listen to the giant Goliath defy his God. He got up and faced the enemy and fought for his faith and for his generation. When we fight the enemy back, we gain more courage and become able to experience healing, prosperity and freedom. We will be able to, like David declare Victory!

36

Issue #8

It's time to put your mountain in check

SCRIPTURE : MARK 11: 22-24

Mountain-------A high elevation of earth.

Commander------The one who is in charge.

Commands---------To give an order or to tell you what to do.

Speak------------------To utter words with a voice.

Physical mountains come in different shapes and sizes. I wondered about these mountains and why some mountains were more difficult than others. There are actual mountain climbers who have record breaking time recordings in the worlds Guinness records. Some make it to the top and some do not. As I researched these mountains, I learned that statistics say that it depends on the mountain. A smaller peak is only 3,000 to 4,000 meters and the air gets thinner, making it slightly more difficult to breathe. The air is also much cooler and drier. Bigger peaks can lead some climbers to have serious respiratory distress with life threatening consequences. The mountains get even bigger and there are 8,000 meter peaks where there is very little oxygen and the human body begins to shut down. Above that altitude the human body is literally dying as the body consumes itself to make up for lack of oxygen. Few humans can withstand this altitude for more than a few days without supplemental oxygen. Amen. Let's list some spiritual mountains: Loneliness, selfishness, depression, anger, adultery, lying, unforgiveness, hate and pride. Even if you haven't done all of them, you have thought about them and that still makes it a mountain. Disobedience, fornication, gossiping, sinning, backbiting, lust and many other mountains. Out of all of those mountains there is still a great mountain that we all have to encounter and that is the mountain of 'Self'. We are our worst enemy. At times we become the hinderance to ourselves; to our blessings, to our healing and to our miracles. We have to get ourselves out of the way and obey God!

The devil has a goal and that is to place a mountain in front of you because he knows that once that mountain is behind you that he has lost the battle.

The Lord, through his son Jesus Christ wants to bless you in every situation you face. He wants all of your needs met, whether they are physical or spiritual, personal or financial because God is a God of more than enough. The enemy on the other hand does not want to see any of your needs met. The enemy tries to keep mountains in front of you, so that you do not progress while you are in the process. He wants to keep you stuck in the same place. I am here to tell you that if you have faith in God and step out of your comfort zone and allow God to work in your life, you will walk in victory.

Choose to believe in God and his word over anyone or anything. Remember God moves when we put our faith and trust in him. God expects us to live by faith. God is waiting for us to speak forth his word back to him so he can move at his word on our behalf.

No one can speak for you. You have to speak the word of God for yourself over your life. Take the first step and speak God's word to your mountain and it will come down and move out of your way. God will begin working in the spirit.

Take the first step in faith and speak God's word to your mountain it will come down and move out of your way. God will begin working in the spirit.

You will soon walk in victory. So don't be afraid to step out and believe in God. Don't be afraid to believe God for even the impossible.

Ephesians 3:20, Proverbs 4:20-22 and Matthew 12:34

So go for it and start commanding those mountains to move out of your path way and stop blocking you from receiving from God.

God is always ready to do a great work in your life but we have to stop being so afraid of these mountains and command them to move in Jesus name. There is power in the name of Jesus. God did not give us the spirit of fear but of love, power and a sound mind.

Open your mouth and speak to those mountains in your life! Stop allowing them to control you and keep you in bondage! The power of Jesus came from the authority of God. All God have to do is speak and it will be done. This is the very point thing God has been trying to get us to do. Walk in authority in Jesus name and speak to that mountain. We doubt God thinking that the mountain is moving by our power and it is not but we have to activate the power of God by speaking his word to the thing that we need to be removed.

41

Issue #9

Its Vaccination Time...

It is time to serve the devil his eviction notice. People of God it is vaccination time. It's prevention time and it's time to serve some eviction notices. There is no more time for these intruders to reside in our homes, in our children, and in our families. Enough is enough!

Vaccination. A vaccination is treatment with a vaccine to produce immunity to certain diseases. It protects us from diseases by making us immune to the disease. Diseases are the cause of death. From the time we were born our country has required of us to receive vaccinations so that we do not get infected with a disease potentially infect others with the disease that we have by simply being in contact with another. Vaccination shots have protected us from Measels, Chicken Pox, Mumps, Whooping Cough and various other diseases. There are also vaccines to protect us from the Flu, Pneumonia, and COVID. These disease just like the devil have a way of sneaking up on you and can reside in your body without you knowing it and then causing death or causing the infection upon another person. For example; you can have COVID and be A symptomatic and then spread the disease to someone else and they experience the symptoms to the point of death. This is exactly how the devil operates in us at times. The enemy will have a person infected with anger, depression, low-self esteem and many other things and it is projected on to others. There are warnings that go out to inform people of the possibility of being infected by these disease. Just like the government uses the media to inform the public of the risk of diseases and let us know whether the disease is airborne or blood borne. The government give us information on to prevent the disease and how to cure if the disease if contracted. The Lord send warnings through his messengers and preachers. To warn people about sin and the attacks of the enemy. As a matter of fact, in the book of Isaiah God told the prophet Isaiah to cry loud and spare not.

> Cry loud, spare not, lift up thy voice like a trumpet, and shew my people their transgression and the house of Jacob their sins.
> (Isaiah 58:1)

Once some of these diseases enter you body they are hard to get rid of. They want to make your body their home. However, all diseases are to be considered intruders. God never intended for the human body to be inflicted with these diseases; but sin taking occasion against man, seized an opportunity. There are some very common diseases such as diabetes, high blood pressure, arthritis, tuberculosis, cancer and other diseases. These diseases are intruders. Just like these physical diseases can be intruders, so can sin and other ungodly activity that we participate in can be intruders. Not only that but oppression and things that come to hold us back such as doubt, fear, and lack of faith. Things that will keep us from getting to our blessing and breakthrough. We have to serve such things an eviction notice. These things do not pay bills. Anything that does not pay you need to go.

There are some things that do pay us but the currency in which they pay may not be godly or align with what God has for us. In this season of our lives, we have to remain vigilant and kick anything out of our lives and our minds and emotions that are not from God.

The CDC which is the center for disease control is an institution that gives the United States guide-lines on how to prevent such diseases or how to treat such diseases if contracted. There is also an FDA which is the Food & Drug Administration. These organizations are responsible for public safety, efficacy and the security of human and veterinary drugs. They teach us on how to protect ourselves using the vaccines.

They tell us what to do and what not to do; What is safe and what not is safe for us. They run test on animals for the safety of human beings. There are always studies on various products to determine the method of safety.

Out of all of the CDC and FDA and the warnings from the government through public knowledge. None of it is 100% able to secure man from harm. There is only one being that can do that and that is God. God can protect us from anything. He can protect us from dangers seen and unseen. God knows what's in front of man and what is behind man. God knows how to keep his creation safe. There is a supernatural vaccine that will protect you from any disease that has ever hit the earth. God's vaccine is guaranteed to work. It's time to tell your intruder its vaccination time and your eviction notice has been served. Tell your intruders that they cannot live there anymore. Tell your intruders that your center for disease control is the Lord Jesus Christ and His Lordship over everything.

Issue #10

Let the Service Begin

Three Questions:

1. What service plan do you have?
2. How is your service to God.
3. What kind of service is God requiring of you?

In this world today, there are so many things going on. There is death everywhere you look. You see it in the newspaper. You see it on the television. You see it on the internet and you hear it on the radio. There is sickness coming from every direction. We don't know when our time is coming but it is coming! So because of that we have to prepare ourselves by purchasing different insurance plans to help protect us and our families. Insurance companies have different plans and services. We get to choose what plans and services we want from these companies and they tell us how much it will cost. Insurance payments are paid either every month or once a year. So, Let the Service Begin!

When we pay people for a service we expect the service to be done correctly. We don't want it to be half done or done incorrectly. In that case we want our money back! You know it just amazes me how God uses natural things to show us spiritual things. Its all in God's plan for our lives. It helps us to understand God better. Come on people of God and let the service begin.

I love it when God tells me something or he shows me something and then turn around and break it down where I can understand the message that he is giving me. When I am really frustrated about something or really, angry and hurt by something, that is when God steps in and shows me my own self.

See God will not show you anybody until he shows you yourself first. He is going to show you the man in the mirror and that is you! This world is looking at you and you have to be careful of what you are doing at all times. God's eyes see everything you do and hears all of your thoughts. There is nothing you hide from God and I mean nothing. If we expect people to service us right, God expects us to service him right!

> For whether is greater, he that sitteth at meat, or he that serveth? is not he that sitteth at meat? but I am among you as he that serveth.
> (Luke 22:27 KJV)

As true followers of Jesus, we also must serve others. Service is helping others who need assistance. Service grows out of genuine love and concern for others demonstrated by someone. Serving allows us to experience the joy and peace that comes from obedience. 1st Peter 4:10-11 says each of you should use whatever gift you have received to serve others. This is faithful stewardship of God's grace in it's various forms that in all things

God may be praised through Jesus Christ. Saints it's time to Let the Service Begin!
Can I share a little secret with you? Serving is a form of worship. A way to express gratitude for what Jesus has done for us and a way to share the love and the grace we've been given. Serving helps us to be more like Jesus. We shift our focus off of ourselves and onto others, through serving. See serving service is in the plan of God. How is your service to Jesus? Allow me to share with you: Service, Loyalty and commitment is high on God's list of expectations for us. There are so many people who think that it is all about what we can get out of God and how God wants to bless us and prosper us. Now don't get me wrong, God does want to abundantly bless us and He loves to give to his people. We get it wrong when our focus is on us and not on God. Just like service is important to us, it is also important to God.

See we have expectations of service and we are disappointed if we don't get it. If God was to issue a survey on your commitment and service, he gets from you. How would you be rated? What backups your service? Your heart or your lips? Isaiah 29:13 says Wherefore the Lord said, forasmuch as this people draw near me with there lips, do honor me, but have removed their heart far from me and their fear toward me is taught by the precept of men. Matthew 15:8-9 Jesus was giving divine insight into the soul of man. Jesus is looking for something in our lives more than just words. He wants us to back up our service with our hearts.

Here is another nugget for you. Our worship will never be right until our relationship with God is right. We can't keep going through the motions and expect God to be pleased with us. We say we want to serve God but do not serve, it will not accomplish anything but empty words! We are only giving God our lip service and pointing fingers on everyone else except looking in the mirror. That's not service at all. We want the pat on the back but no service. Let the Service Begin!

How long is your service plan to God good for? Is it just good as long as God is blessing you with what you want? Or will you be faithful with your service to the end? Can God really trust you with your service? God needs a service he can count on. 1st Corinthians 6:20 says For ye was bought with a price; Therefore Glorify God in your body and spirit which are God's. Our salvation experience costed God his son who knew no sin but had to become sin for us. Our salvation was paid with a high price and our service to God must go beyond just a quick start at the beginning to a solid commitment to serve God to the end.

Matthew 10:22 says and you shall be hated of all men for my names sake: but he that endureth to the end shall be saved. Let me give you something to keep your service in check. You should ask yourself these questions. Am I really committed to God? Am I living out my life with a commitment that is pleasing to God? Am I sharing my faith, studying the word of God, praying and being faithful to God? If you answer no to any of these questions then you need to go and allow God to check you and correct you so that you can be in the right standing with God. There is no more excuses you can use because God knows everything. He knows there will be come struggles and some issues that we will have to deal with but God will help us through all of them. For he has said in his word that he will never leave or forsake us. So, people of God, Let Your Service Begin!

Volume #2

Issue #11

Me and my Big Mouth

Scripture: Proverbs 18:20-21; 'A man's belly shall be satisfied with fruit of his mouth and with the increase of his lips shall he be filled. Death and life are in the power of the tongue and they that love it shall eat the fruit thereof'.

I wonder what comes to your mind when you think of yourself and YOUR BIG MOUTH! Is it something negative? Usually when someone is referring to someone's mouth being big it is usually with a negative outlook.

The mouth is the least thing on the body that is controlled but gets us into the most trouble. As a matter of fact in Proverbs 18:6-7 it says that a fools lips enter into contention and his mouth called for strokes. It says that: A fools mouth is his destruction and his lips are the snare of his soul. In the book of Proverbs King Solomon spoke of the wisdom of God concerning the tongue. The bible calls it and unruly member. We have to learn to get our mouths under control.

BIG MOUTH

Here is the thing. I don't mind one's mouth being big when it is big on the things of God.

When we are studying the word of God, we never know what God is going to show us. It's like getting a surprise gift. Now let's look at what is on the inside of the coin.

Proverbs 18 means that words satisfy the soul as food satisfy the stomach. The right words on a person's lips will bring satisfaction. The word of God is food for the soul. When we feast on the word of God, we become stronger on the inside. The word of God empowers you to stand and be strong against the enemy. The word of God is fuel to our mouth. It makes our mouth a powerful weapon. The enemy knows that when we eat on the word of God, it builds barriers of protection from the enemy. Begin to speak and say: ME AND MY BIG MOUTH!

Proverbs 18 also says that death and life are in the power of the tongue. Go ahead and say that there is Power in my Tongue! This means that our mouth holds something powerful inside of it. We don't have to sit and take anything from the enemy. We don't have to be afraid. We have to stop running from the enemy and began running toward the enemy! We run from the enemy because we don't know the one secret weapon God has equipped us with to fight the enemy. The bible says that we perish from the lack of knowledge. If we don't feast and get fat on the word of God we will lose the battle against the enemy. So study and eat the word of God. It is nourishment for our tongue. Go ahead and feed your big mouth and allow it to be used by God. Our big mouths are the covering of something very powerful. Our big mouths holds our key to victory in every situation we may encounter. Our big mouth can put the devil on the run because he knows the Word of God lives in our Big Mouth and he can't do anything about it.

    With my Big Mouth for healing I called out Isaiah 53:5, For love I called out John 3:16, For Joy I called out 1st Peter 1:8, For Peace I called out Isaiah 26:3, for fear I called out 1st Peter 4:18. And when I can't think of anything to say I will open my Big Mouth and call on the name of Jesus because there is power in that name! There is no other name on this earth that is powerful as Jesus Christ.

Be proud of your big mouth and cherish it and continue to feed it with the word of God and you will never go wrong. For it is only God who can tame our tongue and teach it to war against the enemy!

Issue #12

On The Edge

Scripture: 1st Samuel 30:1-8

The edge indicates an outer limit or the end of something.

An Ephod is a sacred vestment worn by the high priest. It is made of Gold, Blue, Purple, Scarlet and fine twined linen with cunning work. Attached to the Ephod were chains of pure gold and a breastplate of 12 precious stones.

When I read the passage of scriptures, it brought back some painful memories of three different times my home was broken into. Some of the things that were taken could be replaced but there were some things that could not be replaced. I felt like I had been raped and my security was taken from me. My joy was gone. My peace was all gone. I felt so empty inside. My days and my nights were not the same anymore. I used to go outside with my little puppy to allow her to use the restroom and just run and play with her little bad self but I loved her dearly.

My home being burglarized was an attack of the enemy to have me walking in fear. Those burglary's had me walking on the edge. There are certain things in your life that when it happens to you will cause you to be on the edge. When we are on the edge it will cause us to give up and throw in the towel. God can take what the enemy uses to break us and turn it around to make us strong. The enemy is so stupid because God uses Him to make us smarter. To make us wiser and to make us stronger

In the first few verses of 1st Samuel 30, it tells us about David and his men arriving home from their journey. The men find their homes burned down and their families had been taken. These men were devasted and grieved. These men were so grieved that they wanted to stone David.

You might feel like you are on the edge and guess what you are. You are on the edge of your breakthrough. The enemy wants you to think that

God has failed you but He has not. The devil is a liar. God said hang in there. You being on the edge has brought you to the point of your biggest blessing. Stop listening to the lies of the enemy, there is no truth in him.

Sometimes the enemy captures us and keep us in bondage and has us shackled in his rusty chains. God says that even those struggles shall come to pass. There will be a day that you look back on all that has occurred and you will see how the Lord has brought you through it. I shall come to pass! Just like David we have to put on our war clothes and fight the good fight of faith. We have to come out of those self-pity clothes and fight. David put on his war clothes and asked God shall he pursue the enemy. God said purse and take back what is yours. So David went after the enemy and destroyed them and took back everything that belonged to him and more. David had so much that he was able to get spoil for others. God will do it for you! People of God, go and pursue your breakthrough. God said its yours for the taking. Stop waiting for someone else to do it. You go because it is yours for the taking!

I've discovered four things to get you off the edge and to your breakthrough:

1. A burning, which is a cleansing of everything that is not like God. Everything that is hindering

you and have you in bondage. Repent of your sins, You can't get off the edge and to your breakthrough carrying a lot of sinful junk.

2. You have to learn how to encourage yourself because everybody that say they are with you are not.

3. Build. You have to build up your inner man. David spiritual man began to stand up and he sought God. He put on his Ephod and began to war in the spirit of God. You can't fight the enemy naturally. You have to fight him in the spirit of God and by this God moves on your behalf. This gets God's attention and he makes things happen in your favor.

4. Brace yourself for the breakthrough. Get ready and allow God to respond back. It shall come to pass. God is shifting some stuff and you shall recover. God said pursue and you shall win. God said you have suffered long enough. God said healing is yours, pursue and take it by force. Restoration in your finance is yours, take it now! Stop playing with the enemy and take your stuff back that he has stolen from you because your breakthrough is here!

Issue #13

Prisoner of Bitterness

(What are you a prisoner of)?

Bitterness is known in the bible as a spiritual poison and a means by which many are defiled. Bitterness is an underlying problem that doesn't always manifest on the outside but dwells in that person's system. Bitterness is a root. And the root is a source or bubbling fountain that is laying under the surface. It is hidden like the root of a plant. You can see the plant but you don't see the root. The root is hidden under the soil. The same is true with bitterness in a person soul. It is a hidden element that lays under the surface and out of it springs anger and other negative emotions. People who have a root of bitterness finds it easy to get upset over things that others are doing around them. It's like a brewing fountain that lays beneath the surface waiting to fuel something on the surface. Bitterness is a means of defilement. Countless, sicknesses and diseases are a result of bitterness. Unforgiveness leads to bitterness. Unforgiveness that has been in a persons heart for so long can lead to sickness and disease. You must learn to forgive others for their trespasses against you.

HOW TO FORGIVE OTHERS!

Hebrews 12:14-15 says; Follow peace with all men and holiness without which no man shall see the Lord: Looking diligently lest any man fail of the grace of God; lest any root of bitterness springing up trouble you and thereby many be defiled.

Has someone ever said or done something to you and you found it hard to forgive them? Every time their name is brought up, even if it was years ago, it still puts knots in your stomach. When you think of them your heart rate increases and you can feel your blood pressure rising. It is as though you are reliving it again, just thinking about it. If so, you may be a prisoner of bitterness. Being bitter does not affect the person that you are bitter at, it only affects you. Like Frankenstein, bitterness is a monster! A monster turns on hits creator and causes internal damage beyond repair. The person you are angry with has gone on with their life but because of your bitterness and unforgiveness, they hold control of you. Bitterness will affect you until you forgive and give it to God. Many emotions that we feel are not sins. For example: Anger- God says that we can be angry and sin not. However, when anger has overspent it's welcome, it becomes sin. Guilt- is not always sin. Sometimes the Lord gives us a godly guilt conscience and a convicting to get us back onto the straight and narrow. Satan uses guilt to paralyze us in our Christian Walk and when guilt gets out of its cage it too becomes sin. Grief is not always a sin. Grief is a gift from God when used to help us heal from loss or sorrow but if we refuse to allow the Holy Spirit to comfort to comfort our grief it becomes self-pity. Bitterness and Unforgiveness are always sin. Are you in the prison of Bitterness? If you are its time to Let go of it and give it to God so you can be free!

Let me give you six things bitterness will do to your life. Bitterness will devastate you. Spiritually because bitterness will cause you to walk in the flesh and not in the spirit. W have the choice to take a step in the spirit. We can't control what happens in life but we can control how we react or respond to it. If you have unresolved bitterness in your life, you are not right with God and you are not walking in the spirit but in the flesh. Galations 5:22-23 says but the fruit of the spirit is Love, Joy, Peace,

Longsuffering, Gentleness, Goodness, Faith, Meekness, Temperance; Against such there is not law. You can't receive these things if you have bitterness in your heart. You can take bitterness from your list if you walk in the spirit of God.

Galations 6:7-8 says be not deceived, God is not mocked for whatsoever a man soweth, that shall he also reap. For he that soweth to his flesh shall of his flesh reap corruption. But he that soweth to the spirit shall of the spirit reap life everlasting. Yes, bitterness will devastate you spiritually and keep you from growing spiritually.

Do you want to grow in Grace? God is saying if you want to ride this train you have to let bitterness go. Because it is not allowed on this train. Don't get left behind at the station because of bitterness. Bitterness will destroy you. It will destroy you physically. Bitterness has been medically linked to gland problems and high blood pressure, cardiac disorders, ulcers and even insanity. One leading psychiatrist wrote: 90% of all people in the insane asylums could be released quicker if they would learn how to forgive or how to be forgiven. Bitterness discourages you emotionally. Where there is bitterness there is discouragement. It leads to paranoia. You start to develop a victims mentality that everyone is out to get you. You become negative, critical and paranoid You become judgmental of others and think they are always talking about you. Bitterness divide the fellowship. Collision will happen in the church. We have to be careful how we respond to it. When we see it we should seek guidance from God on how to handle it in love. God is our defender when we let go and let God handle it, everything will work out for the good. God allows us to hurt sometimes as a test.

God is wondering if we will remain bitter or become better. God is saying, get over it already! Bitterness will defile your relationship. It will spill over into your relationships and cause chaos. Bitterness is not worth all that trouble. Stop, allowing bitterness to ruin your relationships. Be sure of this, bitterness toward anyone living or dead will destroy your relationship even with the Lord. Bitterness will deprive you of your blessing from God. The enemy comes to steal, kill and destroy. The enemy does not want you to receive a blessing from the Lord. He knows if he can cause you to hold on to bitterness and unforgiveness you will lose your blessings that are right around the corner. Tell the devil he is a liar, and the truth is not in him.

64

Issue #14

Shifted while in the Process...

1. **SHIFT-** To move or transfer from one person, place or position to another. To switch or change.

2. **PROCESS** – Series of operations in the production of something. Series of continuous change or actions leading to a specified end.

3. **PROGRESS** – To move forward or to proceed.

4. **GEARS** – Are a power transmission device

When you start you engine it will run in high speeds about 1500 RPM but if you take that much speed to your wheels, it means your appointment if fixed with God. At the beginning for take off you need more power and less speed and later you need less power and more speed which is governed by gears.

Actually you wouldn't need gears if you had enough engine power. Starting from a standstill position takes a lot of power so the car starts in first gear. When the car picks up speed, initially it helps it keep rolling. So the car is shifted to a second gear. Now you have more speed but less power. In the third gear you still have more speed but less power.

Rolling along at highway speed, you don't need much power. Climbing a steep hill you will need power so the car will automatically shift down and now you can climb the hill. Isaiah was a true Prophet and said God told him to say; And today I am going to tell you what God has lead me to say. The first 39 books of Isaiah tell the people to get their selves in order. By chapter 40 there is a shifting. When you see transition, God is sending a shift in your life and you can't remain the same old person. I want you to look toward heaven and say God shift me. Let's read Isaiah 40:1-5.

Highway is your ticket out of the desert. God knows how to take care of us. Every valley exalted (Money, Self-Esteem, Anointing) God is getting ready to lift you and shift you while you are in the process! Every mountain made low means the high places are coming down. Things that has been out of your reach (Promotion) is coming to you. God is saying that he is going to put it where you can get your blessings! See you are still in the process making progress while God is shifting you. There is a shift taking place in your life. Don't you look at hard times or the hard knocks but know that God is transitioning you to better things and a new place in Him. I promise you that shifts maybe uncomfortable but God is going to pay you double for your trouble. How many of you know that God can? cause opportunity to find you. You may feel like you are stuck today and that it is too late to make your dreams come true, but God is saying No! He is saying I'm about to shift things and doors that have been closed shall open to you. The people that were against you are going to change their hearts and be for you. This is a year of shifting because you have honored God. He is going to put you in position that you could've never attained on your own. It's not just your education, talent or the family you came from. It's the hand of God shifting you to a new level of your destiny. I am not just trying to make you feel good. I am prophesying that a shift is coming to your health, finances and relationships. It may not look like it in the natural, but we serve a supernatural God. He is about to breathe in your direction in a new way. The enemies you have seen in the past, you will see no more. The addictions, the bad habits that are holding you back are being broken and God's favor is being released to you!

The shift is accelerating you higher and to a level you have never been before. God is the gears and he is shifting some people to second gear and some to third gear and some to fourth gear. We all are not in the same gear. God is in control of all the shifting of the gears and he knows what gear to put us in. There is a shift that God has ordained just for you so that you can run smoothly into your destiny.

Issue #15

Stop the Abortion

Scripture: Matthew 13:1-9; 18-23

(1) What is abortion?

A. Abortion is when a pregnancy ends abruptly; either voluntarily or involuntarily and the fetus is expelled from the womb before it can live on its own.

B. Any deliberate procedure that remove or induce the expulsion of a living or dead embryo or fetus.

C. The premature ending or abandonment of an undertaking or destruction of the fetus.

(2) What is a spiritual abortion?

A. A spiritual abortion is the term used to describe people who accept Jesus into their hearts and then really do nothing in their lives that involves Jesus Christ.

B. Spiritual abortion occurs when a person profess faith in Jesus Christ but spiritually "Still Born" which means spiritually dead. It's barely breathing before it's snuffed out, meaning before it's killed.

(3) I want to direct your attention to a very important truth and that truth is that through Jesus Christ we have inherited The Covenant God made unto Abraham.

(4) The book of Hebrews 6:13-15 states that the promise God made to Abraham was made for his seed and not his seeds.

(5) Abraham's seed would be his children would be his children. However, The Promise of God for Abraham's seed to inherit the earth would come through Jesus Christ. Jesus being Abraham's seed and we being sisters and brothers of Jesus Christ; we also inherit the promise. That makes us co-heirs through Jesus Christ. That alone deserves giving God praise.

(6) God has promised to Bless us and multiply us if only we are faithful and put our trust in him. We have to trust him and there is no way around it.

(7) We are a blessed people set apart for God and a peculiar people and surely God has heard the cry of his people in this sinful world.

(8) All who belong to Jesus Christ inherit this promise. God has given all of us this seed which is Jesus Christ and all who have received him is now become impregnated with him. The seed that we are carrying come with many gifts and dreams and future plans from God himself.

(9) Some of us are impregnated with dreams that seems like there is no way that they will come to pass. Then somebody can see their future and the gifts God has for them, but it seems like you always fall short of the mark.

(10) I am here to tell you that we serve a God who knows no limits and has no failures. Don't worry about the fact that sometimes it seems like you can't find your way through because the God we serve is a way maker and he will make a way out of no way.

(11) Stop the abortion! You are killing your baby before it has even had a chance to grow. Stop being so quick to give up on your child because it's the seed God has given you. You are caring a special bundle. So, handle this baby with care.

(12) The enemy want to kill your baby because he knows the threat your baby is going to do to his kingdom. The enemy is intimidated by your baby. He knows your baby is anointed by God and will

destroy every trap he has set. Touch your baby and command him/her to come forth in the name of Jesus!

(13) You have people that don't want to see you blessed with your beautiful baby. Perhaps they have already aborted their baby and they are full of regret and somewhat envy you. Don't listen to the enemy. Don't allow the enemy to trick you out of your blessings from the Lord. God never said having this baby was going to be easy, but it is worth it. So, stop the abortion! Can I tell you that God will make your enemy your foot stool. God will take what was meant for evil and turn it around for your good. What a healthy baby you will have. Oh… how your baby will keep your enemy at bay and keep the enemy trembling with fear. That's why you cannot abort your baby! God has given us something special and right now it's in conception stage. Come on mother's you know what I am talking about. Men you are not left out because God put seed in you also. He is the supplier of these blessed seeds which will become blessed babies. See this is a spiritual thing not a natural thing. So now we begin to feel life and then we can feel it move. No one can see it. This is a spiritual thing not a natural thing. So now we begin to feel life and then we can feel it move. No one can see it but its there. It has started to form and has started to kicking strong where you

can feel it's presence on the inside of you. That thing will give you joy and make you smile, yet no one else can see this thing that God is birthing. God is doing something awesome with you. Just like a natural baby, we have to love it, feed and make sure that it is cared for. What do you feed something that God is birthing on the inside of you? You feed it the word of God. We show it love by keeping it safe from the enemy and we cause it to be strong by feeding and teaching faith. Oh…how amazing it is that God teaches us and breaks things down to our understanding. God is an awesome God and He knows how to get his point across to us. Just like a new mother we must experience the growing pains. There is always pain before we deliver. They say a pregnant woman is in waiting; meaning she is expecting. I don't know about you but I am pregnant with expectation and it looks like you are also.

TO PROPHECY TO THE BODY OF CHRIST :

Somebody is getting ready to birth a financial blessing. Someone is getting ready to birth a new business. Someone is getting ready to tap into the secret things of God. Someone is getting ready to birth a healing ministry. Someone is getting ready to birth a double portion of God.

--------Now Give God Praise Right Now--------------

We should stop aborting the seed that God has blessed us with. Give it a chance to live. Give it a chance to grow. Your baby is alive and well. Whatever it takes to keep your baby alive and healthy do it. Your baby needs love. Your bab needs to hear your voice calling forth in the name of Jesus Christ. Stop being so quick to give up on your baby because Jesus has never given up on us. God has put his seed in us and it is an honor to carry his seed. If God sees us worthy enough to impregnate us with his seed, then it is our job to care of it until it's time for us to deliver. We have to know that God will give us strength to endure the pain that comes along with it.

    In the book of Isaiah 49:1 it says; 'I say so an unborn child is still a person in the eyes of God'. God has called us from the womb. So shall the thing be that God has called from your womb!

Issue #16

What Battle Are You Fighting

PRAISE GOD ! PRAISE GOD ! PRAISE GOD !

    I love it when God comes and download things in your spirit, in your heart and in your mind. DO yall know that there is a war going on? Yes, it is a war going on. Many wars are going on today. And guess what? There is one leader of them and his name is Satan. He is on a mission to destroy God's people. So there is something we need to be doing. There is a war going on and What Battle Are You Fighting?

    Now come on and lets be honest with ourselves. The word of God tells us that we all have sinned and come short of the Glory of God. This is the beginning of how we are going to win our battles.

In the book of Galations chapter Five and verse seventeen it says: 'For the flesh lusteth against the Spirit, and the Spirit against the flesh: and these are contrary the one to the other: so that ye cannot do the things that ye would.' (Galations 5:17)

The flesh and the spirit are always warring against each other and this is why we need to spend more time in the presence of the Lord. God will strengthen us in his presence. The Holy Spirit will keep us ready be preparing us for battle in the presence of the Lord. We have to acknowledge that there is a battle going on and that we need God. The devil and his demons are raging in the earth. In the book of Ephesians Paul tells us that we are in a spiritual battle and we have a very real enemy who has plans to attack us. Ephesians 6:11-12 tells us to put on the whole armor of God so we can stand up against the devil's schemes because our struggles are not against flesh and blood. The devil is our enemy and he is the father of lies. What battles are you fighting, today? Its time for us to be real with ourselves and with others and with God. We cannot win our battles lying and trying to hide it because what's in the dark will come to the light.

God knows it anyway. We have to humble ourselves and go to God. What battles are you fighting? You have to begin to engage the enemy and say things like: Not today devil., This is war!

Say, devil it's on now and you have barked up the wrong tree. I'm learning how to fight in Jesus name. You're going to learn today! Family come on and lets name some of our battles.

The battle of sin, the battle of sickness, cancer, lying, unforgiveness, over-weight, diabetes, high blood pressure, drugs, fear, lusting, adultery, laziness spending time with God, praying, procrastinating, alcohol, slothfulness, deceitfulness, loving our enemy, hatefulness, rejection, come on and let God deliver us today. We cannot go into battle weighed down in mess. We can't enter in God's presence with this junk in us. No, No, No The devil is liar and the truth is not in him!

Family the battle is already won, we just have to learn to walk in our victory! Jesus won it when he died on the cross for us. 1st Peter 5:8 says be alert and of sober mind, your enemy the devil prowls around like a roaring lion looking for someone to devour. The devil is looking to kill and destroy us! He wants to still our joy and our peace, destroy our marriages and use our children against us to harden our hearts. The enemy is behind most church splits and the enemy causes depression, and anxiety. We have work to do family. God is calling us as a church to wake up and take a stand for God. We can't be weak in this battle. God needs us armed and dangerous. We have to be on our walls of intercession and spiritual warfare.

Issue #17

What Water Have You Been Drinking?

Its in the water!

SCRIPTURE : REVELATIONS 22: 1-2, JOHN 4:14

PRAISE GOD ! PRAISE GOD ! PRAISE GOD !

God asked me a question and God also made a statement. The question God asked was; What water have you been drinking? And the statement God made was 'It's in the water'. Now this cause me to do some studying and some searching! This cause me to look at myself! This caused me to check out what I had been putting in my body and allowing to go in my body. I really pondered on the question God asked me and the statement he made to me. What water have I been drinking because it's in the water. I desired to be better. You are going to be amazed at what I discovered. It's so amazing and juicy. It has me so excited that I'm going to share it with you because I love sharing the word of God with everyone.

God had me to write down different names of bottled water. I said to the Lord that I did not have enough money to purchase all of the names of the bottled water. The Lord spoke to me and said get some envelopes because they will represent the bottles of water and get a marker so you can writed what I tell you to write on them. I obeyed God. He then told me to get a few sheets of paper and a pair of scissors, which I did.

Now let's talk about all of these different kinds of water in these bottles. Some of this water is very expensive and some are cheap. Some of the bottles have different shapes and different colors and different names. Some of them have different flavors and minerals in them. Then God really began to pour into me. Wow, God is awesome! See God has his own way of getting our attention. The question is what water have you been drinking because it is in the water! God uses natural things to teach us spiritual things. Can't nobody teach us like God can. God is using these bottles of water to represent our hearts. Thank you, God, for teaching me this! God sees what we don't see and God is going to help us to see today. God, we welcome you to show us today! So, I went to Mr. Yahoo and Mr. Google and let's not forget Ms. Siri. They are all my secret spies and I asked all three of them the same question. I asked them what was the difference between all the bottles of water and what makes one bottle of water better than another? Why some bottle water cost more than others? I asked why some people only drink bottled water and not tap water? I was so nosey that I also asked them what is the difference between distilled water and purified water? I needed to know because God asked me what kind of water was I drinking because it's in the water! I had to find the answer so I could share with others. We need to know because God is trying to tell us something very important. I desire to be better today. So let me tell you what my spies reported back to me. The first thing is that all water have contaminants in them and we can't see them with our naked eyers. The second thing is that all the water go through a process of being filtered to remove debris and bacteria from them. Some leave the minerals in them so it taste fresher.

    Spring water comes with contaminants in it but it also taste fresh and crisp. Purified water comes from other sources that has to be purified. All water come contaminated with something in it.

That is something that I did not know. Bottled water in nice pretty packaging, is not all what people try to make it out to be. Neither the coloring, shape or design or brand of the water can take away from the fact that it is contaminated. It has to be filtered appropriately in order for you to drink it. There have been cases where people have actually died because of contaminated water that was not appropriately filtered enough to make it safe drinking water. Through that, God is trying to teach us that we all were born with contaminants in us because we were born in sin and shaped in iniquity. We can't see it with the natural eye but through spiritual understanding and enlightenment we can see it. God wants to rid us of it before it kills us. We have been drinking all kinds of contaminated water and have not been able to see it because we are blinded from the truth. Don't allow the outside of the bottled water and its packaging fool you. All water is contaminated and has to be filtered enough in order to be safe for you to drink it. Don't allow things to enter your heart without filtering it and ensuring that it is safe for you to consume. That is how you keep you spirit and inner man clean.

Back to the envelops which represented the bottles of water. He said take the paper and cut them into strips of paper so you can place them in the envelops. Take the marker and write these words on them. He said write Hate, Unforgiveness, Pride, Lying, Stubbornness, Fear and many other words. He then told me to place each of them in the envelops and seal them, then mix them up and for me to choose one of them. So, I picked one and I opened it and it said I had pride in my water. I looked up toward heaven and said 'What Pride Lord?'. The Lord showed me the pride that I have in my heart because I did not see it. I have been having a lot of physical issues for a long time that seem to be getting worse. It cause me to have to use a walker, crutches and wheel chair and at times even a scooter. I was ashamed to used them in front of people, especially in church. I would always ask God why me?. The Lord responded by saying Why not you? I would see other people using those help aides but I didn't want to use them. God said what makes you special that you shouldn't have to use them. He said I blessed you with them to help you get around and all you do is complain about them. The Lord told me to shut up and stop complaining and learn how to embrace your situation by trusting me through it all.

That Sunday Morning I preached at my church. I did not know how many people was going to show up when I gave the envelops to be passed out it was the perfect amount. Everyone received an envelop that represented their bottle of water. I told them to open their bottle of water to see what was in their water. They each told what was in their water and was so amazed! They all said it was correct and asked me How did I know. I responded that I did not know but God did. God knows everything thing I shared what was in my envelop and how God had ministered to be about Pride. We all stood up with lifted hands and asked God to forgive us and to continue to help us be better. We have to allow God to continued to show us what is contaminating us. God can always see the trash and the debris and filter it out. God wants to give us better and safer drinking water that has healing in it, Salvation in it, Deliverance in it and most of all have Love in it.

There is one bottle of water that everyone needs and that is LIVING WATER. This is the only water that is NOT contaminated. Once you drink of this water, there will be no need for any other brand of water.

Issue #18

When God is With Us!

SCRIPTURE: ACTS 7: 9-12

PRAISE GOD! PRAISE GOD! PRAISE GOD! IT IS ALL ABOUT GOD TODAY! LORD, WE GIVE YOU ALL THE HONOR AND ALL THE GLORY AND ALL THE PRAISE THAT ONLY YOU ARE WORTHY OF!

Out of one story, God can give you many messages. So, it is with the story of Joseph. The bible tells us that God was with Joseph and Joseph had favor with God! Wow, what an awesome combination to have in your life. We can have the same combination with God. Ask yourself is God with me? Do I have the favor of God? What is it going to take to have that combination in my life. Am I willing to allow God to work on me so that He will be in my life like he was in Joseph's Life? Joseph was one of the youngest boys and he was Jacob's favorite of all his children. Jacob made him a coat of many colors and God would give Joseph these special dreams. Joseph would share these dreams with his brothers. Joseph's brothers hated him and his dreams. Sometimes you can't tell people about your dreams or about your promotions because they are not with you. They want to see you fail and not progress! They don't want you to make it. Joseph was next to the last child. He was close to the bottom and the oldest child was next in line for the blessing but they forgot that God said in his word that the last shall be first and the first shall be last. So, when God is with you, he will refresh your memory of his word because it is hidden on the inside of your heart. Praise God! Go ahead and say God is with me! Joseph's brothers plotted against him and threw him into deep pit and planned on killing him but sold him into slavery instead. Then had the nerves to lie to their father and say that a wild animal killed him. Oh…what great sadness Jacob felt to have lost his son. The Lord was with Jacob and comforted him. When God is with you, you can get through any circumstance or trial or tribulation! Is God with you on today? It is time for us to pick up the mirror which is the word of God and look at ourselves because God isn't going to show you nobody but you! Many times, we want to point our fingers at others when God has been trying to reveal us to us. Don't allow your mirror to be where you cannot see clearly. You need to be in a place of prayer and consecration so that you can see things the way God wants you to see them. When God is with you, you will see truth. God will show you what is really in your heart.

Joseph got sold into slavery, put into prison, and had done wrong but that didn't change his heart toward God. Joseph had a heart after God. See God was taking David to another level in him and that put David in the King Palace. That gave Joseph authority over the King's Palace and put in charge over the whole land. Why? Because God was with him! Stop despising your beginning. Stop despising your circumstances stop despising your trials and tribulation because God is with you. It is time to look up because you been looking down to long. Look up and smile because God is with you and you are not alone. The bible says that God will never leave you nor forsake you! God is not a man that He should lie. Have faith in God because he is with you. God loves when we express our faith in him. Having faith in God will elevate you in him. God will move mountains for the ones who believe not only that God is capable of doing it, but that he will do it for you. God will deal with our enemies. The bible says that God will prepare a table before us in the presence of our enemies. Even your enemies will see you blessed and that God is with you! So, whenever storms come your way, look up and smile at God knowing he is with you. Do not fall for the trickery and lies of the enemy. God is with you!

Issue #19

You don't know the cost of my Praise

Praise means to Worship, Commend, or to give Honor to. Praise is a powerful weapon against Satan. In a sense you can consider praise as a type of prayer. In the bible praise is related to God's awesome power. Praise can make mountains move out of your way. It can make Satan run because he can't stand it when we praise God.

> And David danced before the LORD with all his might; and David was girded with a linen ephod.
> (2nd Samuel 6:14)

The bible says that David danced with all of his might. That means that he exerted all of his strength into praising God. He was praising God with everything that he had. He did not care who was watching him or what anyone thought of him. David's wife was even ashamed of him but she did not know the cost of his praise! The bible says that David was dancing in a linen ephod. Now this linen was very expensive. This was what the chief priest wore. This material was for people of royalty and it was also used for curtains, the veil and screen for the tabernacle. It was associated with special or Holy People. Linen was regarded as a fine gift and was highly valued. Jesus body was even wrapped in special linen. David danced in this fine linen. I regarded the linen because some people have a hard time praising God in their Sunday's Best because we don't want to get it dirty. Oftentimes people do not want to sweat out their hair or makeup. All of those things distract us from praising God and getting into his presence. It will be difficult to got to other levels in God if we cannot worship him on the level that we are on. That means our focus is on us and not on God. How can we be so critical of others who don't mind looking crazy to get in the presence of the Lord. We do not know the cost of what it took for others to come to the house of God and give God praise!

    David understood the goodness of God. He recalled every situation that he had been in that God had delivered him out of. David was a Shepherd and had fought a lion, and a bear. David had been close to death and the Lord spared his life. David had smote the Goliath. David understood how God had brought him out of dark places and into a place of light, a place of revelation and understanding. It was God who was always there for him. It was God who forgave his sins and still saw fit to use him. See David's wife did not know the cost of his praise! David put on his Sunday's Best and gave God Praise! He danced before the Lord. I want this world to know that I love to praise the Lord. I love to worship and to dance in the presence of the Lord. There have been so many skeletons in my closet and many sins that I, myself have committed. I let God down so many times, knowing I was doing wrong but God forgave me and he still loved me. There have been many tears shed that God has wiped away. God took my tears and replaced them with smiles. It is God who keeps me when I am lonely. It is God who heals me of my hurts and pick me up when I am down. It is God who comforts me when I am in pain. Nobody but God understands me! He is the only one who knows me from the inside out. See you don't know the cost of my Praise! God brought me out of darkness and saved me. I wasn't even fit to live and I wasn't fit to die. I was messed up, from the floor up. Jesus brought me out and he gave me life. I can't sit and pretend that I have always been saved because that would not be the truth.

So, go ahead and judge me because you do not know the cost of my Praise! My weave might fall from my head, my suit might get sweaty, my heels may even break off my shoes but you still do not know the cost of my Praise! God has been so good to me. If you do not want to praise God, do not hinder me. Get out of my way and allow me to get my Praise On!!

Issue #20

Don't allow your failures to stop you from serving God...

And we know that all things work together for good to them that love God, to them who are the called according to his purpose.
(Romans 8:28)

Today I am coming from a place of pain, a place of suffering, a place of agony, a place of frustration and a place of turning my back on God! Have you been in either of these places lately? You have tried over and over to obey and trust God but nothing seems to be going the way you need it to go. You are now having second thoughts about serving God and just doing it your own way. Nothing seems to change for the better. I am here to tell you that the devil is a liar and the truth is not in him. I have never read in the bible that life will be free of hard times and struggles. The bible does say that we will struggle for the sake of righteousness. 1st Peter 3:14

says but and if ye suffer for righteousness sake, happy are ye and be not afraid of their terror and neither be troubled. God is saying to not be afraid when the fiery darts comes your way to test you. We have to learn how to rejoice in our suffering and when we are going through our trials and tribulations. We can't allow our troubles to stop us from serving God. That is the trick of the enemy. He wants you to quit and give up on God. Sometimes God allows struggles to come our way because of our sins. God wants us to grow stronger in our faith and become closer to him. He wants us to let our sins go and live for him as his servant. God allows suffering to get the good out of us!

> Let your conversation be without covetousness; and be content with such things as ye have: for he hath said, I will never leave thee, nor forsake thee.
> (Hebrews 13:5)

We all have sinned and come short of the Glory of God. We all have made some bad choices in our life and there were consequences for them. We are supposed to learn from them and become better. God will all the consequence of error to come upon us to humble but he won't leave us. Le us not walk away from God because of the things we put ourselves in. God doesn't walk away from us, we walk away from serving him. God has given us free will to either do wrong or right.

> Now no chastening for the present seemeth to be joyous, but grievous: nevertheless afterward it yieldeth the peaceable fruit of righteousness unto them which are exercised thereby.
> (Hebrews 12:11)

No discipline seem pleasant at the time but painful. Guess what, it will produce a harvest of righteousness and peace for those who have been trained by it. We can learn from our mistakes and start fresh with God! God loves us and he wants what's best for us. He allows struggles to build up our inner strength and faith. God doesn't want us to be weak to the enemy because the enemy will seek to destroy us. So, lets take a stand for God and continue to be servant.

> And not only so, but we glory in tribulations also: knowing that tribulation worketh patience;
> And patience, experience; and experience, hope:
> And hope maketh not ashamed; because the love of God is shed abroad in our hearts by the Holy Ghost which is given unto us.
> (Romans 5:3-5)

This reminds us that even in the midst of pain and suffering, we can see God refining us to make us better servants for him. It's all about humility and realizing we need God everyday of our life. God's desire is to bring us closer to him. If God didn't allow us to go through anything we wouldn't seek him at all. We wouldn't give him any of our time. So we need to praise God for our struggles and failures. It's not time to give up and turn our backs on God because we're going through our trials and tribulations. It is then when we should serve with all of our heart to be the best servant of God!

> And he said unto me, My grace is sufficient for thee: for my strength is made perfect in weakness. Most gladly therefore will I rather glory in my infirmities, that the power of Christ may rest upon me.
> Therefore I take pleasure in infirmities, in reproaches, in necessities, in persecutions, in distresses for Christ's sake: for when I am weak, then am I strong.
> (2nd Corinthians 12:9-10)

Let me also share something else with you. We don't have to do anything wrong and still suffer. Why? Because God wants the world to see his Grace and Mercy. This will cause the lost to drawn to God. God chases after his people because he truly loves them and desire that they be saved. So I leave you with this. Don't quit while you are in the storm. Push forward and endure to the end. God will always be there with you and for you!

Issue #21

Don't Count me out just yet!

SCRIPTURE: 2COR. 4:8-9

> We are troubled on every side, yet not distressed; we are perplexed, but not in despair;
> Persecuted, but not forsaken; cast down, but not destroyed
> (2nd Corinthians 4:8-9)

PRAISE GOD! PRAISE GOD! PRAISE GOD! PRAISE GOD! PRAISE GOD!

I am so excited about today! The devil thought he had destroyed me and counted me out but I am still here! I known that I am not alone in this anymore. Jesus has been with me through it all and he has never left me or forsaken me. Has anyone ever felt like the underdog? I have so many times and it don't feel good. There has been so many people that I consider an underdog. Some may ask what is an underdog? He is a loser or predicted loser in a struggle. This person is a victim of injustice or persecution. People are always quick to put them down saying they will never amount to anything! I am here today to tell you that the devil is a liar and the truth is not in him. I know it's been hard to see your way through but God is going to bring you out. Sure you maybe still stumbling and tears flowing from your eyes but God is going to wipe them all away!

I have learned that underdogs emerge victorious because they have fight in them. They work harder, smarter, and faster than their opponents because they believe they have to. See you have to have an underdog mentality. They are always being underestimated and overlooked. The fight that they have on the inside of them keeps them encouraged. When we study God's word, studying the word of God will keep the fight in you. The word of God will give us the determination to conquer our battles! So, don't count me out just yet!

There were many in the bible who were considered and underdog. One was Gideon, who chose to lead Israel out of the afflictions with the Midianites. He even questioned God because he said I am the least in my family but God told him that (He) The Lord was with him and God called him a mighty man of valor. God said that He will be with you and you shall strike the Midianites as one man. When God speaks that settles it.

What about David, the Little Shepherd Boy. He delivered Israel from the Giant of the Philistines. He was not afraid of the giant at all. He said God has delivered me from a bear and a lion and he will deliver me from you. He said I will cut your head off and guess what, he did just that. Tell this old world not to count you out.

Next, I read about this little boy named Joseph who was hated by his brothers. They threw him in a pit and sold him into slavery. His brothers told their father that he was dead. Oh…but God had put him in the King's Palace and a ring was put on his finger which gave which gave him the authority over the Kingdom! God loves an underdog. He chooses ones considered to be nobodies and make them somebody!

Luke 18:14 says for everyone who praises himself will one day be humiliated before all and everyone who humbles himself will one day be lifted up and honored before all. Humility is priceless in the presence of God. God hates pride. When we humble ourselves and allow God to have his way in us and through us because victory is already ours.

Now there is an underdog that is more than any underdog that I know. He was obedient to his father and humble as a Lamb. He knew no sin but gave his life for the sins of others. He was the underdog of second chances. He was all wisdom and made us more than conquerors. This underdog loved us all and he forgave us of all of our sins. There is nobody like this underdog. My desire is to be all that He (God) is calling me to be! His name is Jesus Christ. He was beaten and bruised. He was hung and stretched wide, thorns put on his head and spear was put in his side. The devil counted him out but Jesus said no don't count me out just yet because I still have some work to do for the father. He rose back up in three days with all power in his hands and he conquered death and took the sting. Jesus asked death 'Where is your Sting?'

Tell your enemies 'Don't Count me out just yet', because I am on a mission for God! I might be going through some trials and tribulations but don't count me just yet. Family and friends may have turned their backs on me but don't count me out just yet. I may have lost loved ones along the way but don't count me out just yet. Yes, my body is aching with pain and doctors can't help me, but devil don't count me out just yet because of Jesus Christ I walk in VICTORY! I am not defeated! I am who God says I am! Thank You Jesus for saving me!

Notes

Notes

103

Notes

Notes

Notes

Made in the USA
Columbia, SC
16 July 2024